Made in the USA
Coppell, TX
22 July 2024

34922328R00069